Rebellion Box

Hollay Ghadery

Rebellion Box

radiant press

Copyright @ 2023 Hollay Ghadery

All rights reserved. No part of this publication may be reproduced, stored in a retrieval system or transmitted, in any form or by any means without the prior written permission of the publisher or by licensed agreement with Access: The Canadian Copyright Licensing Agency (contact accesscopyright.ca).

Editor: gillian harding-russell
Cover art: Camilla Gibb
Book and cover design: Tania Wolk, Third Wolf Studio
Printed and bound in Canada at Friesens, Altona, MB
Second Printing 2023

The publisher gratefully acknowledges the support of Creative Saskatchewan, the Canada Council for the Arts and SK Arts.

Library and Archives Canada Cataloguing in Publication

Title: Rebellion box / Hollay Ghadery.
Names: Ghadery, Hollay, author.
Description: Poems.
Identifiers: Canadiana (print) 20230196098 |
Canadiana (ebook) 20230196101 |
ISBN 9781989274910 (softcover) | ISBN 9781989274934 (EPUB)
Classification: LCC PS8613.H33 R43 2023 | DDC C811/.6—dc23

radiant press
Box 33128 Cathedral PO
Regina, SK S4T 7X2
info@radiantpress.ca
www.radiantpress.ca

Table of Contents

1 • Postcard, Santa Maria
3 • It won't stop, but it will be divided into four stages
4 • *Maiasaura*
6 • Dreadnoughtus
8 • Mom
9 • Mammalian Attachment Theory
10 • Heifer
11 • RUN
12 • SPIN
13 • ROLL
14 • Rumination
15 • Drunk Dream
16 • Patient 31
19 • Yepsen
20 • 20K
21 • Psychomachia
26 • Good People
27 • Search History
28 • The 13th Step
29 • Cosmic Script
31 • Braids
32 • Pouch of Douglas
33 • Ovum Ghazal
34 • *Zendegee Khālee Neest*
35 • Walk it Off
36 • Cronartiaceae
37 • Anemic Galaxy
38 • Apeirophobia
39 • Runaway Universe
40 • Hunting Season Selfie
41 • Zeigarnik Effect

43 • Cold Comfort
45 • Rebellion Box
47 • Slipped Earth
48 • Corpse Pose
49 • Chair Pose
51 • The Limits of Whiteness
52 • Foster Memorial
53 • Why Fatima Killed Her Mother
54 • Water Safety I
55 • Water Safety II
56 • Water Safety III
57 • Felt Cute, Might Delete Later
58 • shadow pocket
59 • Texas Sharpshooter Fallacy
60 • Instructions for Lucretia
61 • Fight Like a Girl
63 • *Arosak*
64 • Free Indirect Discourse
65 • Optical Phenomena

Postcard, Santa Maria

1.

Across the pool
the boy's plum-
dark eyes gulp
refracted light
all over the girl
beside me.
Stretched
to indifference

her thighs are
perfectly fattened
calves, flicking
flies; their frisson
of velvet shimmers

made slow
by this
drugged heat.
Made soft.

2.

I'm not that girl
anymore. I
have the
conviction
of dust and

*the cervix
of a fifteen-year-old,*
my doctor says.
Not bad
for four kids

so I believe
in anything
so I can
believe
at all.

3.
The boy is coming
snake sway
in his hips, a
roving satellite over
breast and
breath, and brown.
His

air-
compressed confidence
warps the children's
laughter

baffles the sun
so even the girl
looks up.

4.
I'm not that girl
anymore—
her curling toes,
her eyes

impossible beyond
shades, her weight
inside me, shifting
my embarrassment
of cliches,
scattered
like nail clippings.

It won't stop, but it will be divided into four stages

Deny it. Then make a link between Count Dracula, a 15th-century Wallachian voevode named Vlad and someone

    who doesn't love you back.

Grieve. Then deny it. There's brutality in speculation—Dracula hunched over heaving cleavage. Vlad issuing orders, twenty-thousand Turkish women, children, and men impaled. Someone saying,

    No, I don't smoke anymore.

Acknowledge tendency. It's vicious, it's closer. Can't say for sure Vlad inspired Dracula but he did flay, cannibalize, and bury people alive. Bodies scattered over kilometres of vacant land. Brutal, like someone stepping out onto the street with someone else,

    lighting up.

Accept it. Not all accounts of Vlad portray him as psychopathic. In parts of Romania, he's a hero. Others lump him into the same category as Ivan the Terrible and Genghis Khan, his tyrannical behaviour more or less standard for the time. More or less

    a better-looking version of yourself. They're on the street laughing and it's more or less
    ruthless

    but it won't stop. You will be divided.

Maiasaura
('Good Mother Lizard')

She poured her grape juice
on a freshly-hatched chick
and if there's one thing I know,
it's there's no
coming back from that.

Breathing is

taken for granted but it's not
always an involuntary act.
I can see her eyes fill, but
hear no in. There's no out. I'm
tempted to soft-pedal
truth into her

three-year-old mind
with the gravitational pull
of God, but if there's
one thing I know, it's that
heaven's too abstract and for
now, the three of us are tangled
in different stages of stunned.

I pick the chick up and wrap it in a
tea towel, its body twitching. I don't
want her to be afraid to sleep at night,
don't want her to rethink the kindness
of sharing her drink with a friend, but

I also don't want her to live without
understanding of consequence—cause if
there's one thing I know, it's that she'll try.

There's something to be said
for ready-to-run hatchlings.

The chick
is still and she touches its head, softly
says, *Sorry
'til I die.* It's a whisper,
an inhaled spasm as I pull her to my lap.

She nuzzles her wet cheek against my heart,
and if there's one thing I know, it's
there's no coming back from this.

Dreadnoughtus
(*for Joe*)

runs
deeper
than interest

blooms bird brains,
bone maps,
metric tons
of
timeless

devotion:

doesn't know
fractions
but will recite
the bite force
of 29
pre-
historic
predators

doesn't buy time,
says,
they're
not in the world
any longer, but

they're not
in the past
either

they're taking up
space, everywhere

and if
you can't see
that, you need
to think

bigger.

Mom

Coming and going
I'm all the same
to you. An
umbilical tug,
a reference to

measure the pluck
of seconds
until your life begins,

coming or going
staying or leaving me.

Mammalian Attachment Theory

how am I
supposed to live if
it means nothing:
my lips, perfect
in the seashelled
cradle
of her foot, her
sonic squeal
when she sees
my face—

what if
we're not made
for each other

just by
each other

are only
predisposed
by vagus fire,

bound

by cells
responding
to other cells?

Heifer

I want to see
what I couldn't see
the first time. See
with the slow gaze
of cattle, their genuflect
feyness.

I want to feel

what I wouldn't
feel before. Summer

a banner,
flowing out of me;
a cloven moon,
setting.

Sunflowers

following light, west
to east. A rewind
time lapse
of the difficult

births
of us all.

RUN

Realizing I'm weeks late, we run
to the pharmacy, five minutes before closing
to buy a test. The cashier asks if we want her
to double-bag it, and you say,
No—
You say,

*That's what I
should have done.*

SPIN

They say they do it because of the w a y
                    their skirts f l o a t,
                                  because of how they've u s e d
                    their own force to t u r n
one thing into something e l s e.

ROLL

Nana runs a black tourmaline rolling pin over
the back of her hand, her skin warm and
smelling of curled
orange peel

her bones
having cradled
having crumbled,
having said,
I'm afraid

this is the
way it goes.
Your body betrays,
and will continue
to betray you.

Rumination

I could hang myself
from the balcony
of every thought

but I try to regard
them with the tender
disdain of cats
try

to think

clear

as bottle-brushed
veins, calm

as the conversation
of pine boughs

Drunk Dream

Waking
into the chirpy pink
eye of a cactus flower
you know

where your children are
you remember
last night
your mouth salivates
freely and
your brain is a white
light
bubble

even if
your antelope heart's still
kicking,

you're
sober—a dull
word
for this state
of grace.

Patient 31

The story is already starlight:

a member of a fringe church
infected thousands with a virus

and you're no
spatio-temporal specialist,
but snowflakes

scurry
like late theatre-goers
at three a.m.
when you wake to the echo
of this tale. You were

half-listening the day
you heard it on the news.

You'd stood
in the living room

looking at the baby's toy
farm on the floor:
chickadee chatter and
your children's laughter
rising

from the yard
like the scent of apple
bread you'd baked
for lunch

and you know
your children are
getting older, so

you lie
in the night
trying to remember
the last time you looked
into their eyes,

really looked—
and you calculate
the time between inhale,

exhale,
and compare it
to how much time
you may have left.

Yepsen
(for Charles Schweder)

Burn blisters from the woodstove
the whole of my dog's snout. A
frost-shattered axe blade and the
fine thread between what I want
and the ditch of sky. The fine line
between my silence and splinters
in my palm

A mouthful of thistle

The burden of indifference, difference:
indefinite standing. A bird's eye view
of the shoreline and a pocket
book of birds. A gift, the blood
of my ancestors. The burden: the fork
in my blood. The fine line between
being who I am and getting what I want

20K

I trust the system that
fuels gunpowder guts,
grass-fed thighs, 170
beats per minute, and

I'm going strong, so bone
dust fine I'm moving clearly
for movement's

sake. Going strong, so
sunshine slick the eye
of the earth dilates
around me. For God's
sake, I'm so tired, so
pulse point sure

that I trust the system,
its ecstatic silence, my
fine ideals and body's
breakneck laugh, bone-
marrow-deep, little-kid-
filthy and gorgeous.

Psychomachia

I'll never feel
like my old self again,
so there's no question
of suffering
blooming amaryllis or
laughing like
the last luxury on earth. I can't

picture a wall free of fingerprints,
a sink without beard clippings.

And my milk-stained existence rests
on that spider
until morning
comes, stretching crimson
arms around the house. I
trace

daybreak,
the cloud-on-cloud action
and hone in
on a little light, growing.

It's all I need
to be less
bothered by this
knotted bewilderment,
deep as newborn blue
and mobile bright.

My friends live
in their soundstage cities,
smile like quicksand. They
call and I say,
*Cut me a slice
of your dishwater sky—*

I know they're forgetting me. That
I've forgotten home, flushed
with gifts: a new world welcome.

*

It's a battle
to control the rate of absorption—
the rate
the days
consume me:
their tiny eternities
carrying over and
over themselves like
my daughter's blonde hair,
braided over
her shoulder, a stretch of sky
so wide

I could reach in, pull
out sunlight, strand by strand.

I'm a dazzling succession
of maybes and missed
appointments. A good-
for-nothing wife
with unruly thighs in the
hardware store.

Aisles with chainsaws,
ropes
or rat poison
                                              bring to
mind empty rolls of toilet paper and socks
shoved between couch cushions,
                                              bring to
mind visions of the baby in black, imported
kegs of my husband's favourite beer,

and me:
                a butterfly,
pinned and
untouchable.

Don't tell me
you know
your own soul
so well.

Friends call and listen
to my lakewater heart leaking,
the white buzz of early
autumn and

I'm trying to understand:
there's still red in the trees,
not my son's hair,
anymore.

It's my fault,
                I know. I wished
       it away.

*

As usual, the clocks are sick
with this dusty disconnect
between waking and sleep
and the baby
          dozing
half-awake in my arms—she's
just
a feeling
in the ends of my hair...

The baby—my blue-eyed
                    black hole —
reminds me we were all
very small
once;
we woke
our mothers early, blinking
sparks, slingshot
smiles;

reminds me
to love
the natural disorders
of my body,
but the afternoon throws itself
across
the yard, an angry toddler.

Still, when I breathe out, she's
beside me breathing in,
and she keeps
me going.

When friends call, I say, *Everything's
fine*, and laugh
canopies of razor blades
                    in every room.

I close my eyes and
see sharks in the ocean, their
oil-spill eyes
                dripping, close
        my eyes and can still
point to the sun.

    *

On the way back from school,
we find a rubber alligator
in an oasis
of cream soda, and I begin
to think all good stories are
anonymous.

We stand in the sweet hook
of a crab-apple tree and the
afternoon
       falls
               eyelash
                       heavy.

It's what I wanted: baby
swaddled against my chest,
one
small hand in
each of mine, walking home,
talking
about the taste of clouds,
where the wind comes from,

if it ever finds its way home,
and I know
no matter how close I hold
my children,
no matter how I plan to keep
them safe

there'll never be enough blue
sky in the world, not when
I'm through with it.

Good People

You've been busy.   Why—
...don't you own a TV?   Does
...your husband need a hobby?   It

...must be a religious thing, a   matter
'bout birth control. An accident.   They're
...all from the same father, then?   Loved

When you used to hang out more—   We're
...just saying, this has gotta' be the last   (Good
thing—you can get rid of it.   People

used to have to live with their mistakes)

Search History

brown discharge, white mucus
spotting 10dpo
geriatric pregnancy age
does having kids reduce risk of breast cancer
does having kids reduce risk of ovarian cancer

why was the *Triceratops* sick in Jurassic Park
can you get genital herpes from a cold sore

allergies earache
allergies itchy skin
allergies perimenopause
is 40 too young for perimenopause
how many kilometres in 7156 steps

what are the odds of my husband dying before me
who wrote the theme song for *Murder, She Wrote*

———————————————————————.

The 13th Step

fresh crinkle of summer,
bent ray of
waterlogged light,
the darkest fish under
the dock

a scorched birthmark
on my father's chest,
tectonic skull tickle of
daisy chains
of dandelions,
my best friend's
buttercupped chin

my shoeboxed faith
in the mouth of every tulip
in windy-day leaf tangos,
in the penny-perfect slot between
my mother's front teeth

in strawberries, sun-soaked
and bursting between fingers
like something
still alive
from all the ages
through which I've passed.

Cosmic Script

Your daughter knows darkness
        is just the absence of light,
                and flowers drink sunlight and rain to grow. She knows
her dog's nose print
                is unlike any other dog's nose
                              in the whole world
            and that a newborn's skin is thin
as rice paper.

But she doesn't know what happens when she dies,
            and it keeps her up at night, her stomach pinned
                    in a rollercoaster drop.
                  Her thoughts,

                        a hundred rubber balls
                        bouncing
                        around a rubber room.

A natural extension of your body, she
finds you
                in darkness and climbs into your bed. You tell her
about comets: their tails spanning star systems.
                Their bodies huge snowballs of gas,
            dust
                      and ice that orbit the sun,
pulled back from their aphelion orbits millions of years
                                after they set out.

Who knows where they go.
                    Who knows what they see.

It could be anything.

                                        It's okay not to know for sure.

　　You say that, but you're
                              not   so sure,
                                      yourself.

Braids

I don't know if we're meant for the stars but I still
like to hear his voice, see pictures of him, maybe
his wife, now and then. A handful of things to
wake me. Like sun stains. I used to

like to hear his voice, see pictures of him
lying with his hair in braids, then using
his wife, now and then. A handful of things to
help me here. I'm alive. I'm static. I'm

lying with his hair in braids, then using
the sun to part the trees and the trees to
help me here. I'm alive. I'm static. I'm
not listening to him breathe. I've designed

the sun to part the trees and the trees to
give way. Sure, he may pull through but I'm
not listening to him breathe. I've designed
an answer. The answer to everything is to

give way. Sure, he may pull through but I'm
not meant for the stars, or braids. I've designed
an answer. The answer to everything is to
hear his voice. See pictures of him, maybe.

Pouch of Douglas

only the soft ping
of a cosmic ray
from some collapsed
star can reach; the
point is

it can expand
to accommodate growing
things, and you can only
feel it when something
is wrong

when that point of light
around which your vast
collection of
little worlds revolve
jinks.

The point is
to remind you

you had no say
you were given
this name
when you were
nothing

to remind you
to live, anyway

Ovum Ghazal

spawned the moment one person exists inside another
like Russian nesting dolls, this fairytale isn't another

story hinging on the hero traversing hostile terrain
to make you whole, make you enough. The other

stories that try to tell you this lie. The truth is you've
always transported wholeness within you; there's no other

force. Only the undulation of your being, the
waft and pump of completeness you bring. Other

paradigms will persist, but you're limited in number not
possibility. Something to consider, one way or another.

Zendegee Khālee Neest
('Life is not empty')

Say it won't get me
anywhere, but regret is a
baby tooth rooting

upward. It gives me
something
to work against,
the violence

of interpretation:
from black and white to
baffled blue crabs pooling

in sponge cells and how—
all of my life—I've gathered
my stories like dust.

Walk it Off

Not doing this again—
the sky fat with lakes,
and lakes fat with skies;
hawk parallax mimicking

a sky fat with lakes
and lunatic ivy in my
veins mimicking the
plummet of stars

down to the lake, a
fistful of obsidian ivy

a hawk mimicking
heart parallax.

Cronartiaceae

Something about me says
the ever-loving green of you
must go.

My spore stages and all
my blister-swell and all
my rust wheeze and all
my indiscriminate snacking
says

everything in me wants to live,
too badly.

Anemic Galaxy

The thing that makes me
is the near-absence of everything else;
                        makes me

    slave to the holy swell of morning,
                    its prism cover. The near-absence
of everything makes me
reflexive, mostly. One chemical kick into existence
and I was born starving. "Einstein once said
'time-space is eating up matter'"
        and I don't know what that means,
                  "…but I do know
                            something
    is eating up time."

This makes me
        eager to please.

Apeirophobia

You'll learn about galaxies. Of
how you have infinite life to live. How

old you are by observing the energy
you radiate into space. In space

you'll require no air or substance
to carry you along, but along

you'll go, a compressed calm of calm
compression, radiating through emptiness

though emptiness is a dream for
a swollen universe and the universe

is a future that's dying of
loneliness, because you prefer

the past—it's predictable, and
in it you have infinite life to live.

Runaway Universe

No matter which way we look in space,
            I owe You some kind of explanation
We see billions of galaxies rushing from us—
            I ran at short intervals, to keep a sense of proportion
A person in any other world would see the same thing:
            Do you realize, I wonder, what submerged
            identities we women can have?
A universe expanding at breakneck speed
            To practice the restraints of civilization,
            not explore its possibilities
And the faster the runaway, the greater the shift —
            What to do with my freedom now I've stolen it?

Hunting Season Selfie

Thick fur and thin hide
we share, so tell me, what's bear
for: *live and let live?*
Kill only to survive. Get
your kid off my carcass. My
life isn't your photo op.

The Zeignarnik Effect

For the record,
it's not the Fat Cities,
beers on tap
closing shift blues
or names of regulars
I remember most—not

even the one
who brought me
bear meat from his
hunting trip, even though
I'd said, *No, no
thank you.* And
no, I won't eat that

not because it's   meat
but because it's   bear

and how he'd looked
puzzled
a moment before
breathing, *Ahhhhhhh,
I see.* But Makwa won't
hold survival
against you.

What I remember is
the busiest
weekend of summer,
tables packed, my
gilded reflection floating
in the bar's l o n g, disilvered
mirror while I poured

drinks, left them huddled
and sweating on the
glass rail

how I'd said
nothing, not even
No thank you,
when a waitress
put in an
order and said, *Don't
rush this one.
Not like Indians
fucking tip
anyway.*

Cold Comfort
(in response to Flight 571)

"Guilt matters. Guilt must always matter. Unless guilt matters,
the world is meaningless."
—Archibald MacLeish

Don't feel bad. Nothing
                              will ever
be as complete as Mom's garden:
                              the bumper crops
                              of beans, green
peppers, squash. Or Dad's store:

toggle bolts,
anchor bolts, carriage
bolts. Everything
                in a different size,
everything
in place. Don't worry.

Bite flesh off bone,
like any good prince. As with
                any good olive,
your teeth scrape stone. Soft
and keen as the spot
above your right ear, the
                give of skull, of glass
                into flesh. It's
easy. But God,

it's cold. The sky's turned bone
                        -crushing blue and the mountain's
                        got
this twisted metal grin.

God knows, it's strange,
but I sleep fine, eat
                  readily, and smile
                        for the camera.

You can get used to
almost anything. God

     saw fit
                to give me eyes near the top
of my head, so I can watch
                      my step and
catch the mountains disappear upwards,
Colgate clouds pour into pockets
of sky. I can see

and it's all very surprising, but it's got
nothing to do with me.

Rebellion Box
(Fort Henry, Kingston, 1837)

Ask your husband about the honey bees. I may
have an affinity for things that drone and drown
out. On the way here everything was so green, it hurt
the trees practically threw themselves on the road
and to think, only days ago I'd been worried about
my nose most of all. Now, John's been hung and the rest

of us rot and cut away at stove wood. Just rest
and fleas for the foolish. I know some of us may
have stepped into battle thinking only about
valour, liberty, winning. It's easy to drown
in these abstracts but it's a dangerous road
to follow. I've seen how brave men hurt

so easily. Tell Mary I think of her often. It can hurt
to think of myself like this: all stone and soot, but rest
assured my present circumstance is not finite. Every road
leads home. It's true, our troops sat in that tavern and may
have felt some degree of foreboding already. We drown
our fear, glass after glass. I admit I was afraid to think about

Mary. Home. Honey bees and my broken nose, about
to fall off my face from want of attention. I know I hurt
the most remarkable people. God, Mary. I will drown
my primitive conditions. I've managed to create. I rest
in dirt and root myself to the root of her. I may
be the most pressing of hopeless things, because road

after road and I still brandish youth like a shotgun. Road
after road leads to finding something to do about
all this time on my hands. I dovetail my work. I may
be the most diligent of craftsmen. All this time can hurt,
weigh black and blue in the middle of my face, the rest
—the luxury of a blue cotton dress—the rest can drown

like marzipan creek pebbles, July's sweetgrass chew. Drown,
and wait, because all that talk and rallying—it cleared a road.
I won't stand for futility. There are so many reasons to rest
your beliefs here, and not one of us has. I write home about
paying debts on time, mending the fence. I write to avoid hurt,
boredom—being forgotten. I write you about the bees. You may

remember the summer we cleared your husband's land. May
came hard and the bees came early. I was stung twice. It hurt,
but Mary was in blue, and it was something else to think about.

Slipped Earth
(for John Gillespie Magee Jr.)

Fly cracked-rib sky, spent
red and orange
      at your feet, pinched
heart, concrete eyes. Bury
      your lighthouses, spend
days sunward. Want burned
      blue. No
trench talk. Want fast, like
      slick grass, a bomb-drop kiss,
a mouth to say,
      I miss your face.

Corpse Pose

at least there must always
be hands

clasped in prayer
dry and distant mountains
ears open next to eyes and

fleshy parts to hold, like
God's final thought before bedtime
how it hangs, clipped.
I was born nostalgic

just looking out my window—*gheir az
khuda hichkas nabood*—
legs folded under me,
my cupped palms hold
no secrets—
one cannot
panic

quitters never rest or
regain the upper hand
so what if I begin
to cry despite myself? I
used to wish to
vanish. Now I
wish for a
xenagogue
yeki bood, yeki nabood
Zion is air rustling in my lungs.

Chair Pose
(Uxbridge Grammar School, 1852)

They're fine monsters,
on a physical level. Unruly
bones, feet
splintered downwards.
Nothing between them
and disobedience
but a good teacher.
Think about it.

One

good punishment
might be to line them up
against a wall, have them hold
a deep-seated position,
nothing between them
and the floor but empty space.

Think of a specified time

and stick to it. It's grounding,
another good way to keep
your chest broad, heart lifted.
Of course, they will writhe
from discomfort,
and pain

it's certainly challenging.
You will require balance,
course, and determination.

Just think:
You're extending their fingers
to the sky, rooting
bones and feet in smooth
inhale,
exhale. In
possibility.

Think
of pain as beauty,
of this as a good way
to fine-tune your monsters.

The Limits of Whiteness

...do not
behave, mostly
loophole
themselves, they

understand

race is
active-struggle,
is
forged agitation,
is
Aryan jetsam,

race
is becoming
           by force

Foster Memorial

You were gone, so I stopped thinking about getting old.
Instead, I thought of light flooding India, lifetimes spent in peeled
sunshine and how Ruby used to wake up laughing. It's true, I
think about immortality, about living better in anticipation, the

thought of light flooding India, lifetimes spent in peeled
marble, stained glass, Indiana limestone. So, I'll grow young
again, cap the sky, keep you safe. And me, I'll wait for
water-lily eyes, azure temples, arching intentions. I'll use

marble, stained glass, Indiana limestone so I'll grow young:
it's how you'd remember me. I'm afraid I've seen too
much of the world without you. All sinew and insinuation.
It's made me raw. I still shave my face clean, cuff my pants—

it's how you'd remember me. I'm afraid I've seen too
little of tribute, may have misjudged the size of the sky.
Still, I'm honest. I forget birthdays, appointments, but
I went to India and saw your face, an azure temple.

Why Fatima Killed Her Mother

I got to know how *yen pok* smells cooking
                              before I was five,
how pomegranate tastes, plucked
                              from the top of a tree
by my mother's hand, each seed,
                              each
                              drop of blood.

And there wasn't a time
I didn't know what a *prick looked like*,
how it felt to be broken in
                    by edge of knife,
        by back of knife,
as with a blue tattoo, connecting
my eyebrows in a line.

See, the old woman was always lying,
                          and *I know it would be good
if I could say how awful it was, how
crime doesn't pay*,
but I spread my sheets and
                      they're covered with ash and pilaf. I open
my legs and spill
                rosewater.

Water Safety I

It wasn't the water or fear of drowning. I still carried the memory of my amniotic weight. It was my teenaged instructor: smooth and bulge-blossomed in his swim briefs, nothing like my dad's soft silver back heft. I sat on the side of the pool and sobbed until my mom said we could go home. On the way, she bought me fries at McDonald's and I licked the salt off my fingers while she cooed, *See now? All better. Wasn't that a silly way to behave?*

Water Safety II

So much
for pathetic fallacy,
the night dilated
clear. It
didn't matter

that I had a buddy;
he had a buddy too,
slash mouthed
and pulpy eyed.

It was a surprise,
waking up in a body I
hadn't been dreaming in

all I wanted to be
was less
to stare at,

a sign
for him,
not me,
that read:

Remember,
checking her pulse
is not the same as
receiving consent
and

drowning people do not
splash and shout.

Water Safety III

The week's been a shovel
but today's grey-break has
the kids stridulating
summer

so we head to the pool.
The first
to arrive, it's
a quivering bowl of
blue Jell-o
and we want to
jump

but stand shoulder-
to-shoulder instead,
toes clutching deep-
end edge
and review
the basics:

before we dive,
what dangers should
we look for?

Wires
        rocks
                logs

the bloated corpses
of our enemies.

Felt Cute, Might Delete Later
(for Lucy Maud Montgomery)

Not a Cavendish shoreline in sight, just
shadows yawning tall as angels in the garden
                                                    crocuses
each small as a baby's thumb, and I'm posed
on the porch, flounce
                    of summer
                                    in my skirt.

Hard-boiled sun and barbiturate blue sky are asleep
in my bones but I'm still predictable in my demand
                                                for more.

So tell me what it's like to stay asleep
                        after the dream ends—not a Cavendish
shoreline in sight
—and how to exist in a tide;
                how sometimes you fight, and sometimes
                              you let it take you places.

shadow pocket
(for LMM)

she wanted to sleep with me
and at last, I knew the truth: wild
and weird as an opium dream,
born under the curse as another girl
might have been born cross-eyed,

but I went to her—silly goose had
the bed fitted out like a bridal one
to lie with me spoon fashion. And I've

been feeling my devil
again, slimy, unclean, and about the size
of a matchbook sitting over my heart.

Texas Sharpshooter Fallacy

("It has not mattered much what anyone else thought. I will always try to catch and express a little of the immortal beauty and enchantment of the world into which I have sometimes been privileged to see for a moment."
—Lucy Maud Montgomery)

It has not mattered much what anyone else thought.
I will always long for a little illusion; those old
evenings when I'd lie there peeling the moon. I
had no name, just an amniotic glow. Don't ask how

I will always try to catch and express a little of our
atomic ruin and fashion it into a weapon of life—
anything to give sense to my scuffed eyes, clear
knees. I've become uncomfortably cautious of

the immortal beauty and enchantment of the world into which
I've been born. It's fresh as it ever was, just further
out of reach. But you either have faith or you fall, so I
collect my tear salt and—be still my bleating heart—

I have sometimes been privileged to see for a moment
so clearly, I could slice open a cherry blossom vein with
surgical precision. I could draw a circle around my wild
fire and call myself a sure shot.

Instructions for Lucretia

Dash his brains into his mouth
Map the stretch marks on your thighs
Call your mother, talk about the day you were born
Admit to nothing
Open the window and roll the sun between your fingers
Laugh until it hurts
Until you cry
Cry
Measure your comfort in crow miles
the distance between your life and honour
Slice open the underbelly of every cloud
Let it rain
Let them drown

Fight Like a Girl
(for Lexi Kaufman)

Now I don't go
fighting, not
without the sun
in my throat.
Got form,
sure,
but favour
formlessness.

Still float,
aim
and miss
some days.

Meaning:
at least I try.
If I fail,
it's more than
I can say
for lies,
loss

betrayal,
funny thing—
feels

like devotion, feels
like eyes look
then opt for
pointlessness.
To assail

without cause
is a fist, like a
clause, should stay
open until impact,
stay prone. And
sure

I've got my
restlessness
but I don't go kicking it
across the street
like a stone.

Arosak
(for Adele Wiseman)

life is limited
to what you're alive to,
so even the doll is
happy to be created

doesn't know
you're not supposed
to be dazzled
by pimp's packaging
or the carrot
of the future

Free Indirect Discourse
(for Atefeh Rajabi)

                                  exhale, your sway
of body, saffron
sunrise
                                              neck tilt to Caspian Sea

see
no one told you
                    how silence hangs
                        like unclaimed
                            hours, like

      unnamed
                    sleepers, like night
              dozing, its back
            to you

and you,
          you loved this world so
                          inhale, no one

    can tell you

           when you are born.

Optical Phenomena

("What does one do with such a thought? With all the panic and the rage? Everywhere I look I see ice melting while everyone else hops into their cars and orders their takeaway and flies off to Ibiza, all the silent deniers believing life can go on as usual. One night I woke up screaming out of a dream about a tidal bore of ocean water pouring over me."
—*Blaze Island,* by Catherine Bush)

Look, I see ice melting
while everyone else hops
into their cars and orders
their takeaway

and I wish
I could pretend
it's not happening too—
but I
can see ships disappear below
the horizon; can
recognize each of my children
by the way they thrash
in their sleep

I feel it coming strong:
the dull self-absorption
of ocean liners, and

I wish I could pretend too,
but different stars
are visible
from different latitudes

and the lovers of the world
are wrong: we don't all share
the same sky; we are separated
by more than we think

the dull self-absorption
of sunburnt tourists at swim-up bars
tipping staff with mini-bottles of shampoo

thinking skating on slob
ice proves the world is cool. The
cataract sky, clear. The earth-weep,
distant and the worlds of ocean,
clean.

Notes:

"Heifer"
This poem was inspired by *Night Watch: The Vet Suite* by Gillian Wigmore (Invisible Publishing, 2021) and was, in a previous form, an experimental review I wrote for CAROUSEL Magazine.

"Yepsen":
The Old English word *"yepsen"* refers to the amount that one can carry in two cupped hands. I first encountered the word in George Eliot Clarke's *Canticles II* (Guernica Editions, 2020), and thought it was a marvelous way to measure the things that we touch and grasp in our everyday lives. I made note of the word, and then it came to mind again when I was reading P.G. Downes' *The Sleeping Island: The story of one man's travels in the great barren lands of the Canadian north* (Coward-McCann, 1943) since there is so much tactile description in his writing

Downes' description of Charles Schweder—the son of Fred Schweder, a Hudson Bay Company manager posted at Windy Lake—was particularly interesting to me since, like myself, Charles was biracial (in his case, Cree and European or white). Downes writes with an inquisitive and astonishingly sensitive interest in Charles' mixed-race identity, especially considering the book was written in 1943. Downes ruminates on how being biracial may mean having different sets of expectations placed on you. Having experienced the pressure of biracial, bicultural expectations myself as a person of Iranian/British mix, I decided to dedicate this poem to Charles.

"The 13th Step":
The last three lines of this poem are a slight rephrase of a line in Adele Wiseman's *Old Woman at Play* (Clarke, Irwin, & Company, 1978), a book of nonfiction in which Wiseman explores the creative process through her mother's prolific doll-making. "One of the characteristics I have noticed in creative people is that they retain about them something still alive of all the ages through which they have passed" (p.12).

"Cosmic Script":
This poem is a poetic adaption of a chapter in *Fuse*, my memoir of mixed-race identity and mental illness (Guernica Editions, MiroLand, 2021). The chapter deals with comforting my daughter during an episode of severe anxiety about her own death while also trying to reconcile myself to it—an endeavour that proves extremely challenging as I live with existential OCD: a form of OCD where one experiences repetitive and debilitating thoughts about death, and what comes after it.

"Pouch of Douglas"
Also known as the recto-uterine pouch, the Pouch of Douglas is named for and by Scottish anatomist James Douglas (1675-1742). There is a list of parts of the female anatomy named after European or white, male scientists, including "fallopian tubes," "the G-spot", and "Cooper's ligaments."

"Ovum Ghazal":
This poem was inspired by and uses sentiments from "The macho sperm myth": "The idea that millions of sperm are on an Olympian race to reach the egg is yet another male fantasy of human reproduction," written by Robert D. Martin and published on the online newsletter, Aeon.co, August 23, 2018.
   https://aeon.co/essays/the-idea-that-sperm-race-to-the-egg-is-just-another-macho-myth

"Zendegee Khālee Neest":
"Zendegee Khālee Neest" ("Life is not empty") is the first line from "Dar Golestāné," a poem by contemporary Persian poet Sobrab Sepehri.

"Cronartiaceae":
While exploring the flora and fauna on our property, one of my children took a picture of me using *Picture This*—an app that identifies plants. The app identified me as Cronartiaceae, which are a family of rust fungi made up of some serious plant diseases that can cause mortality in conifers.

"Anemic Galaxy"
Italics are an observation made by Lucy Maud Montgomery in her 1930-1933 journal on November 18, 1930. *"Einstein says in a recent pronouncement that 'Time-space is eating up matter.' Perhaps he knows what that means. I don't. But I know something is eating up time."* (L.M. Montgomery's Complete Journals, *The Ontario Years (1930-1933)*, edited by Jen Rubio. Rock Mills Press. 2019, p 93).

"Runaway Universe":
The lines on the right are excerpts from *The Book of Eve*, by Constance Beresford-Howe (McClelland & Stewart, 1973). I consider the novel a personal feminist manifesto.

The lines on the left are excerpts (though not always exact excerpts) from *Our Universe*, by Roy A. Gallant (National Geographic Society, 1980), pp. 245-246.

"Zeignarnik Effect":
Named after Soviet psychologist Bluma Zeigarnik, the Zeignarik Effect refers to the theory that people remember unfinished or interrupted tasks better than completed ones. Many people experience intrusive thoughts and anxiety that come with these unfinished tasks that have the effect of reinforcing memory.

"Cold Comfort":
"Guilt matters. Guilt must always matter. Unless guilt matters, the world is meaningless" is a quotation from Archibald MacLeish's 1958 play, *J. B.* (Houghton Mifflin, 1958), a modern retelling of the story of Job.

Flight 571 is the Uruguayan Air Force flight that crashed into the Andes on October 13, 1972. Some sentiments in this poem were adopted from *Miracle in the Andes*, written by Nando Parrado and Vince Rause (Crown Publishers, 2006).

"Rebellion Box":
Rebellion Boxes were carved by prisoners kept at Fort Henry, Kingston during the Rebellion of 1837. These tiny boxes were made from stove wood that the men there created to pass the time and to keep them focused on their cause. Often prisoners sent their boxes home to loved ones.

Joseph Gould, a Quaker, prominent businessman, and political figure in Uxbridge Township (then in Upper Canada), fought in this rebellion and was imprisoned in Fort Henry, where he made a Rebellion Box, which I learned about while visiting the Uxbridge Museum. Mary was his love interest, whom he eventually married. Since it would have been considered improper, he did not address his letters from Fort Henry or send his rebellion box directly to her. Instead, he wrote to Mary's mother, asking about everyday happenings on their farm and obliquely inquiring after Mary.

"Slipped Earth":
This poem is a response John Gillespie Magee Jr.'s war sonnet, "High Flight." Magee enlisted in the Royal Canadian Airforce in 1940, and trained in Ontario. In November 1941, he saw action in Lille, France where famous German Fighter pilot Joachim Müncheberg shot down and killed all Magee's section but him. A little over a month later, Magee was killed in an accidental, mid-air crash while training over England. He was nineteen years old.

"Corpse Pose":
This poem is an abecedarian and erasure poem that uses Ava Farmehri's *Through the Sad Woods Our Corpses Will Hang* (Guernica Editions, 2017) as its base text.

"The Limits of Whiteness":
The title is inspired by Neda Maghbouleh's *The Limits of Whiteness: Iranian Americans and the Everyday Politics of Race* (Stanford University Press, 2017). This book examines the roots and influence of the 'Aryan myth' which holds that Iranians are Aryans—and therefore white—against the lived experience of Iranians in America, where they are treated as distinctly not-white.

"Foster Memorial":
The Foster Memorial is a Byzantine-inspired mausoleum located outside Uxbridge, Ontario erected by Thomas Foster, a former mayor of Toronto, in 1936 in honour of his daughter, Ruby, who died just before her tenth birthday of pneumonia, and his wife, Elizabeth, who died a few years later of an undocumented cause.

"Why Fatima Killed Her Mother":
This poem uses lines and sentiments expressed in two texts: *My Mother's Persian Stories* by Saeid Shammass and Shaunie Shammass (Moshe Alon, 2018) and *Storyville, New Orleans: Being an Authentic, Illustrated Account of the Notorious Red-Light District* by Al Rose (The University of Alabama Press, 1974). The lines in italics are from an interview with one of Storyville's former child-prostitutes.

"shadow pocket":
Lucy Maud Montgomery had an admirer, Isobel, who was in love with her and doggedly sent Maud adoring, highly sexual letters, which repulsed Maud. Nevertheless, they did not stop her from visiting Isobel and, on one occasion, sharing her bed. That Maud—a minister's wife—strongly suspected Isobel was a lesbian and found this "lifestyle" to be an aberration, but continued to write to Isobel is interesting. That she doesn't sever ties reflects either a broadminded gesture or a secret interest.

Some sentiments in this poem are taken from LMM's 1930-1933 journal.

"Texas Sharpshooter Fallacy":
The quotation is from *L.M. Montgomery's Complete Journals, The Ontario Years (1930-1933)*, edited by Jen Rubio (Rock Mills Press, 2019), p.26. On March 1, 1930, she wrote, "I have written to please myself. It has not mattered much what anyone else thought. I have always tried to catch and express a little of the immortal beauty and enchantment of the world into which I have sometimes been privileged to see for a moment—the moment of 'Emily's' 'flash.' Those who never have that glimpse cannot believe there *is* such a world. I can but pity them."

"Arosak":
"Arosak" is the Farsi word for doll. This is an erasure poem from Adele Wiseman's *Old Woman at Play* (Clarke, Irwin, & Company, 1978). As mentioned in the note on the poem, "The 13th Step," this is a book of nonfiction in which Wiseman explores the creative process through her mother's prolific doll-making.

"Optical Phenomena":
The epigram is a quotation from Catherine Bush's novel *Blaze Island* (Goose Lane Editions, 2020), p. 174.

Acknowledgments:

Rebellion Box was over a decade in the making, and there are many people to thank for their support and guidance during this time.

To Elizabeth Greene, George Logan, Erin Foley, Lucy Black, Jacob McArthur Mooney, Margo LaPierre, Jennifer Hosein, and Mary Ellen Csamer, thank you for your kind words and encouragement. Thank you to everyone in my MFA poetry workshop who helped shape some of these pieces.

To gillian harding-russell, thank you for your expert eyes and the gentle push to look deeper and distill further.

To Debra Bell-Kennedy and everyone at Radiant Press, immense gratitude for believing in this scrappy collection.

Thank you also to the Canada Council for the Arts and the Ontario Arts Council for their generous funding of this project.

Finally, so much love and appreciation to Mom and Dad, Matthew, Joseph, Fionnuala, Soroor, and Harvey for putting up with me while I fiddled with words instead of spending time with them.

Individual poems have been published in the following journals:

"Rebellion Box," *The New Quarterly* (Issue 164, Fall, 2022).

"Fight like a Girl," *West End Phoenix* (June, 2022).

"Roll," *CAROUSEL* (June, 2022).

"Texas Sharpshooter Fallacy," Felt Cute, Might Delete Later," and "Runaway Universe," *The Temz Review* (Fall/Winter 2021).

"*Arosak*," *longcon magazine* (Issue 9, 2021).

"How Fatima Killed Her Mother," *untethered* (Vol. 6.1, 2021).

"*Yepsen*," *Understorey* (Issue 21, Rural & Remote Living, 2021).

"20K," *The Quarantine Review* (August 9, 2021).

"Instructions for Lucretia," *Understorey* (Issue 20, Spring 2021)

"Cosmic Script" and "Apierophobia," *The Antigonish Review* (Issue 204, Winter 2021).

"The Foster Memorial," *Grain* (Vol. 47, No. 3, Spring, 2020).

"Psychomachia," *The Malahat Review* (Issue 196, Autumn, 2016).

"*Maiasaura*," *Grain* (Vol. 43.4, Summer 2016).

"Cold Comfort" and "Chair Pose," *The Fiddlehead* (Issue 252, Summer, 2012).

"Braids," and "It won't stop, but you will be divided," *Grain* (Vol. 36. No. 3, Spring 2009).

Hollay Ghadery is a multi-genre writer living in Kawartha Lakes, Ontario on Anishinaabe land. She has her MFA in Creative Writing from the University of Guelph. Her fiction, non-fiction, and poetry have been published in various literary journals and magazines. *Fuse*, her memoir of mixed-race identity and mental health, was released by Guernica Editions' MiroLand imprint in Spring 2021. *Rebellion Box* is her debut collection of poetry.